CENGAGE Learning

Poetry for Students, Volume 28

Project Editor: Ira Mark Milne Rights Acquisition and Management: Vernon English, Jocelyne Green, Aja Perales, Sue Rudolph, Robyn Young Composition: Evi Abou-El-Seoud Manufacturing: Drew Kalasky

Imaging: Lezlie Light

Product Design: Pamela A. E. Galbreath, Jennifer Wahi Content Conversion: Civie Green, Katrina Coach Product Manager: Meggin Condino

For product information and technology assistance, contact us at **Gale Customer Support, 1-800-877-4253.**

For permission to use material from this text or product, submit all requests online at **www.cengage.com/permissions.**

Further permissions questions can be emailed to **permissionrequest@cengage.com** While every effort has been made to ensure the reliability of the information presented in this publication, Gale, a part of Cengage Learning, does not guarantee the accuracy of the data contained herein. Gale accepts no payment for listing; and inclusion in the publication of any organization, agency, institution, publication, service, or individual does not imply endorsement of the editors or publisher. Errors brought to the attention of the publisher and verified to the satisfaction of the publisher will be corrected in future editions.

Gale
27500 Drake Rd.
Farmington Hills, MI, 48331-3535

ISBN-13: 978-0-7876-9892-8
ISBN-10: 0-7876-9892-X
ISSN 1094-7019

This title is also available as an e-book.

ISBN-13: 978-1-4144-3833-7
ISBN-10: 1-4144-3833-8
Contact your Gale, a part of Cengage Learning sales
representative for ordering information.

Printed in the United States of America
1 2 3 4 5 6 7 12 11 10 09 08

Self-Portrait in a Convex Mirror

John Ashbery 1975

Introduction

Written in a style often described as verbal expressionism, "Self-Portrait in a Convex Mirror" is the title poem in the collection for which John Ashbery won a Pulitzer Prize, a National Book Award, and a National Book Critics Circle Award, all in 1976. Originally published in 1975 in the collection *Self-Portrait in a Convex Mirror: Poems*, the lengthy title poem was inspired by a painting by the same name, completed in 1524, by the Renaissance painter Francesco Mazzola (1503-1540), who is most commonly known as Parmigianino. The poem is viewed as Ashbery's most accessible in terms of language and style and therefore distinguishes itself from many of Ashbery's other poems, the style of which has often been regarded as unconventional in the extreme. Indeed, many of his other poems have been described as being difficult or impossible to decipher. "Self-Portrait in a Convex Mirror" is counted among the masterpieces of late-twentieth-century American poetry, and it is certainly regarded as Ashbery's personal masterpiece. The work is ostensibly a meditation on Parmigianino's painting, offering lengthy observations on Parmigianino's artistic technique and skill. It also delves into themes such as the nature of art, poetry, and artistic expression, and explores such philosophical issues as the nature of personal identity and the soul. The poem is available in *Self-Portrait in a Convex Mirror: Poems*, published by Penguin Books in 1990.

Author Biography

Born in Rochester, New York, on July 28, 1927, to a fruit farmer and his wife, John Ashbery spent his youth in Sodus, New York, a small town near Lake Ontario. When Ashbery was thirteen, his nine-year-old brother died of leukemia, an event that scarred his childhood with tragedy and loss. Ashbery attended Deerfield Academy and in 1945 enrolled at Harvard, developing friendships with the poets Frank O'Hara and Kenneth Koch. After earning his bachelor's degree from Harvard in 1949, Ashbery began his graduate studies at Columbia and New York University, where he focused on French literature. His circle of friends at this time included artists and painters, one of which was Jane Freilicher, who illustrated Ashbery's first publication, the limited edition *Turandot and Other Poems* (1953). In 1955, Ashbery was awarded a Fulbright scholarship to study in France; he became an art critic and correspondent in Paris. While in France, Ashbery wrote two poetry collections (*The Tennis Court Oath*, published in 1962, and *Rivers and Mountains*, published in 1966), both of which were regarded as highly controversial. This was due in part to the experimental form and style of the poems.

Returning to New York in 1965, Ashbery worked as executive editor of *Art News*, holding the position through 1972. Soon after his return to New York, he published the volume *The Double Dream of Spring* in 1970. This was followed by *Three Poems* in 1972. By the mid 1970s, Ashbery was receiving a greater amount of critical recognition for his poetic work and was regarded as one of America's most prominent poets, despite the controversy surrounding his work. He additionally worked as an art critic for both *New York Magazine* and *Newsweek*. In 1975, Ashbery's "Self-Portrait in a Convex Mirror" was published as the title poem in his collection, *Self-Portrait in a Convex Mirror: Poems*. The volume was praised for being more accessible than some of Ashbery's earlier work. The acclaimed volume received the Pulitzer Prize, the National Book Award, and the National Book Critics Circle Award in 1976.

From 1974 through 1990, Ashbery served as Professor of English and a Codirector of the M.F.A. program in Creative Writing at Brooklyn College, and as a Distinguished Professor from 1980 through 1990. During this time, Ashbery continued to write poetry. His works *Houseboat Days* (1977) and *As We Know* (1979) were increasingly described as both difficult to decipher and avant-garde (avant-garde is a term applied to artwork that is viewed as obscure, intellectual, and experimental). Since then, he has worked as the Charles P. Stevenson, Jr., Professor of Languages and Literature at Bard College (in Annandale-on-Hudson, New York). His more recent work includes *And the Stars Were Shining* (1994), *Chinese Whispers* (2002), *Where Shall I Wander* (2005), and *A Worldly Country* (2007). Ashbery's body of work includes poetry, a novel, plays, and essays, and he has received numerous awards and prizes for his achievements, in addition to those bestowed upon *Self-Portrait in a Convex Mirror: Poems*.

Poem Summary

Strophe 1

"Self-Portrait in a Convex Mirror" opens immediately with an explanation of Ashbery's subject. In the first strophe (a distinct division within a poem that is similar to a stanza), Ashbery describes the method by which the Renaissance painter Parmigianino created the painting known as *Self-Portrait in a Convex Mirror*. With short, vivid phrases, Ashbery outlines the way Italian painter and architect Giorgio Vasari (1511-1574) discusses the creation of Parmigianino's convex mirror itself from a sphere of wood. Ashbery catalogs details of the portrait, the way the quality of the light ensures that Parmigianino's face looks life-like, the way the curve of the mirror and its reflection is captured by the artist. Embedded in these technical details are Ashbery's observations on the soul he perceives animated in the eyes Parmigianino has painted. "The soul," Ashbery says, "establishes itself;" yet it "is a captive," longing for freedom, but trapped within the human form; and the human form is trapped within the sphere of our world, "life englobed." Ashbery's extended ruminations on the position of the soul within the body and within the world give way to a return to the technical discussion of the artistry of the portrait. Commenting on the distorting effect of the convex mirror in Parmigianino's painting, Ashbery studies the size of the artist's hand. These observations yield quickly to a meditation on the nature of our perspective of reality: "The whole is stable within / Instability," Ashbery states.

Strophe 2

In the second section of the poem, Ashbery begins a more serious digression from the subject of Parmigianino's painting. His concentration is broken: "The balloon pops." His thoughts wandering, the narrator thinks of his friends, conversations he has had with them, and the ways in which parts of others—their thoughts, their ideas— are absorbed by the self. We are "filtered and influenced" by others in the same way that light is changed by "windblown fog and sand." The self, like art, like nature, is all collaboration. Ashbery meditates on the shifting nature of the world around us, likening Parmigianino's portrait to a person at the center of a sphere. The narrator then describes the vision that passes before one's eyes to reality spinning about a central core like a "carousel starting slowly / And going faster and faster." In trying to capture an instant of this spinning, Parmigianino has been only marginally successful, the narrator notes, observing that it is impossible to record a perfect moment, to "rule out the extraneous / Forever" or to "perpetuate the enchantment of self within self."

Strophe 3

Ashbery, in the third section of the poem, continues to consider what it means to contemplate a painting such as Parmigianino's, particularly when one understands how much more challenging it is to actually capture and express experience. Being able to put *today* into perspective is nearly impossible. The present, the narrator observes, is pregnant with promise and potential: "Even stronger possibilities can remain / Whole without being tested." The pattern of opposition Ashbery explored in the first section is repeated again, as he discusses the flow of potential contained within a room. Such a place, he notes "should be the vacuum of a dream" but instead is continually replenished "as the source of dreams." Once exposed to reality, a dream is forced to try and thrive in a place that "has now become a slum." At this point, the narrator refers once again to Parmigianino's painting, or at least Renaissance art scholar Sydney Freedberg's discussion of it. Ashbery relates Freedberg's analysis of the portrait's use of realism to project disharmony rather than truth. The argument feeds the narrator's discussion of the distortion of dreams and reality. This section of the poem is concluded with the idea that while the nature of dreams shift as they are "absorbed" into our reality, in this process "something like living occurs."

Strophe 4

In the fourth section Ashbery employs Freedberg again to comment on Renaissance art, and the place of Parmigianino's painting within the art of that time period. Ashbery discusses the care with which Parmigianino captured the effects of the mirror's rounded surface upon the artist's reflection. The narrator observes how, in studying the portrait, it is almost easy to forget that the reflection the painting captures is not your own. The effect is one of displacement once the realization that it is not your own reflection is made. Such a startling response is likened by Ashbery to the bizarre experiences of one of (nineteenth-century fantasy and science fiction writer) E. T. A. Hoffmann's characters, or by looking out of a window and being startled by a sudden snowfall.

Strophe 5

Ashbery in the fifth section of the poem begins by briefly relating biographical facts about Parmigianino, how soldiers "burst in on him" during the sacking of Rome (in 1527, by troops of the Holy Roman Emperor Charles V), and spared his life. From Rome, Ashbery moves to Vienna, "where the painting is today" and on to New York, which he views as "a logarithm *Of other cities."* *Ashbery recounts the history of the creation of the portrait, as well as his own creation of the poem in New York. Ashbery's short cataloging of the details of city life is a reminder of the way he interacts with the portrait, is drawn to it, and is then drawn back again to his own reality, his own creation, forcing the reader into the same flux of attention. This section of the poem transitions the reader away from the artwork of Parmigianino again; the* narrator states "Your argument, Francesco, Had begun to grow stale as no answer *Or answers were forthcoming.*" Yet Ashbery leaves open the possibility of a continued relationship or exchange with the painting, suggesting that perhaps "another life is stocked there In recesses no one knew of; that it *Not we, are the change; that we are in fact it* If we could get back to it." This recalls Ashbery's earlier statements about dreams, and the shifting nature between dream and reality: trying to recall the impact a work of art has had on us is similar, Ashbery seems to be suggesting, to the struggle to recollect a fading dream.

Strophe 6

In the final, lengthy movement of the poem, Ashbery turns decidedly to his own creation, having highlighted both the limitations and possibilities of the aesthetic (set of artistic principles) of another artist. Released from the fixed point to which it had been previously anchored, that is, from Parmigianino's portrait, the poem now embarks on a more loosely structured, philosophical exploration of the themes Ashbery has previously touched on, such as the soul's response to art, and the reality of the present moment. "No previous day would have been like this" (l. 382) he states. "I used to think they were all alike, *That the present always looked the same to everybody." As he does earlier in the poem, Ashbery emphasizes a point by pursuing opposing ideas. The reality of one's interpretation of art, and the inspiration it offers is questioned, but accepted as having a place "the present we are always escaping from* And falling back into." Conscious of his own position as an observer, as a person interacting with a piece of art, and that the reader of the poem is in the same position, Ashbery has stressed throughout the poem that a person in such a position is not *exclusively* in this position. That is, the art admirer and the reader of a poem have a place in a reality, in a life in a city, that is separate from, but a part of, their interaction with the art work. "And we must get out of it even as the public *Is pushing through the museum now so as to* Be out by closing time. You can't live there," Ashbery states. He goes on to express the limitations he sees inherent in artistic expression, limitations centered around the impossibility of capturing the truth of a moment in the present. The effect of such an effort is always "the 'it was all a dream' *Syndrome, though the 'all' tells tersely* Enough how it wasn't. Its existence / Was real, though troubled," Ashbery states.

Self-Reflexivity

"Self-Portrait in a Convex Mirror" is a work in which the poet examines, through the course of the poem, his own act of creating poetry. This is known as self-reflexivity, and it features prominently as both theme and device in Ashbery's poem. The work is very much *about* its own self-reflexivity. Repeatedly, Ashbery calls attention to the creation not just of art, but of *his* creation of *this* work of art. Additionally, he discusses that this is being done in other works of art as well, particularly in Parmigianino's self-portrait. In the Parmigianino painting, the artist calls attention to the methods by which he accomplished his artistic achievement by having selected such a peculiar format—a painting of a reflection. Furthermore, the mirror is not a simple flat mirror, but a convex mirror. The choice appears to have been made for the sake of artifice alone. Ashbery also notes that Parmigianino's is "the first mirror portrait." Ashbery's own self-reflexivity can be observed in the statements he makes throughout the poem. Repeatedly he refers to his own actions, nestled as they are within his descriptions of Parmigianino's portrait and his reaction to the work. His attention wandering, he notes "I think of the friends *Who came to see me, of what yesterday* Was like" and then uses this as a bridge back to the poem. His memories of yesterday intrude "on the dreaming model *In the silence of the studio as he considers* Lifting the pencil to the self-portrait." He draws attention back and forth, from the painting, to his own life, and back again to the artwork that inspired his meditation.

Coming back to his own perspective, Ashbery not only comments on his own response to Parmigianino's painting, but discusses his creation of a poem about it. He speaks of the exact present moment of writing, in "New York *Where I am now.*" *Ashbery emphasizes his continued desire to derive meaning and substance from art*: "I go on consulting This mirror that is no longer mine *For as much brisk vacancy as is to be* My portion this time." Ashbery's self-reflexivity is demonstrated through his fascination with *today*, with his attempts to depict the truth and meaning of the present moment, and his willingness also to portray his process. "All we know *Is that we are a little early, that* Today has that special, lapidary *Todayness.*" "*I used to think they were all alike,*" *Ashbery goes on:* "*That the present always looked the same to everybody.*" He speaks then of being drawn back, as if down a corridor, toward art, toward the painting, wondering what "figment of 'art'" it is trying to express, then suggests "I think it is trying to say it is today." *The expression of, and experience of the present moment is conflated with artistic expression when Ashbery observes that* "Today has no margins, the event arrives Flush with its edges, is of the same substance, *Indistinguishable.*" *He also meditates on the failure of art to convey that which the artist intends, and in doing so calls into question his own ability to accomplish the same task. "Often" Ashbery says, "he finds* He has omitted the thing he started out to say / In the first place." In pointing out our "otherness" as a viewer of art, he emphasizes the existence of the reader of his poem, of the reader's perception of his own art.

Topics for Further Study

- Research the historical event (referred to by Ashbery in "Self-Portrait in a Convex Mirror") known as the Sacking of Rome, which occurred in 1527. What political circumstances preceded this event? What effect did this military occupation have on artists living in Rome at the time? What was the state of Rome following the attack? Write a report on your findings.

- Browse through an art history text, such as Frederick Hartt's *Art: A History of Painting, Sculpture, Architecture*, and select a painting that you respond to strongly, whether positively or negatively. Compose a poem about the work. Include some physical details about the work itself as well as observations about your emotional response to it.

- Examine the works of Parmigianino (other than *Self-Portrait in a Convex Mirror*) and other Mannerist painters, such as Correggio. Be sure to examine Mannerist sculptors, such as Cellini, as well. Observing their styles, their distortions of perspective or exaggeration of features, sketch or paint a self-portrait emulating the Mannerist style.

- In the sixth section of "Self-Portrait in a Convex Mirror," Ashbery mentions *Mahler's Ninth*, and how it was said that a portion of this piece invoked the sentiment of awakening a moment too late. This is an allusion to the composer Gustav Mahler (1860-1911) and his ninth symphony, the last symphony that he completed before his death.

Listen to this symphony (available in the collection *Mahler: The Complete Symphonies*, 2001) and write a brief essay in which you explore why or how such music serves as a source of artistic and philosophical inspiration.

Isolation and Connection

Ashbery quotes Italian painter and architect Giorgio Vasari's claim that Parmigianino set out to copy all that he saw, which was, Ashbery notes, "Chiefly his reflection, of which the portrait / Is the reflection once removed, *The glass chose to reflect only what he saw* which was enough for his purpose: his image." What Ashbery notices about the painting is that the artist in fact depicted only the distorted largeness of his own person ("the right hand *Bigger than the head, thrust at the viewer"). The background, save for a glimpse of the window, is practically empty. The artist himself is the entire world, or globe of the poem, one that is organized* "around the polestar of your eyes which are empty Know nothing, dream but reveal nothing." The self that Ashbery describes portrayed in the painting has become symbolically isolated, by its own hand, from the rest of the world. The artist's own self-involvement has led to its isolation, Ashbery seems to be saying, whereas his own work of art, the poem, seeks to use art to identify connection, to the world, to reality, to a consciousness of the present moment. While Parmigianino's portrait is encapsulated and isolating, this very nature of the artwork prompts Ashbery's philosophical meditations on his own reaction to art, and his place within his own world, which, conveyed to the reader, is an invitation to do the same. Parmigianino's isolation inspires Ashbery's attempt to connect himself to *today*, to his life in New York, which he describes. Through his interaction with the artwork, and his understanding of the possibilities of the reader's reaction to his poem, Ashbery emphasizes both the isolating and connecting nature of art.

Style

Mannerism

The term Mannerism refers to an artistic style beginning to be popular during the later years of the High Renaissance (a period of advanced artistic achievement) in Italy, during the early 1500s. Mannerist works of art were highly individualistic and featured distortions of perspective and qualities that were artificial or exaggerated rather than naturalistic. Parmigianino's *Self-Portrait in a Convex Mirror* is itself an example of a Mannerist piece, and Ashbery's poem has similarly been described as Mannerist for its own distortions of perspective: the reader is in effect viewing Parmigianino's portrait from Ashbery's point of view, which is shaped by his own intentions. Like Mannerist paintings which drew attention to themselves as artificial creations through exaggeration, Ashbery draws attention to his own work of art by examining his own act of creating it. It should be noted as well that some scholars view Ashbery's technique as a critique of Parmigianino's Mannerist work. While both pieces are works of self-representation, Ashbery strives to analyze Parmigianino's as well as his own methods of self-portrayal, thereby distinguishing his approach from Parmigianino's by his attempt to eliminate not the self-reflexivity of the work, but the narcissistic and limiting qualities he finds in the painting.

Expressionism

Ashbery's style in "Self-Portrait in a Convex Mirror" is sometimes referred to as expressionistic rather than Mannerist. Expressionism, or verbal expressionism, is the literary equivalent of the artistic abstract expressionism, in which the artist intentionally uses elements of distortion to create a desired emotional effect. The artists Jackson Pollock and Pablo Picasso were among the best known abstract expressionists. The purpose of verbal expressionism is the conveying of emotional truth, rather than the statement, in linear, traditional ways, of logical arguments or ideas. In "Self-Portrait in a Convex Mirror" Ashbery so accurately discusses Parmigianino's painting, he in effect offers a glimpse into the emotions expressed in the painting, presenting the verbal equivalent of viewing the painting itself (or the experience of viewing it), which transcends the mere description of the painting's details. In doing so, Ashbery delineates the possibilities of both verbal and visual modes of expression.

Pop Art in 1970s New York

When "Self-Portrait in a Convex Mirror" was written in 1975, visual art in New York was under the influence of several movements, including that of Pop art; Ashbery was, in fact, friends with one of the best known Pop artists of the time, Andy Warhol (1930-1987). A visual artistic movement that began in Britain in the 1950s, Pop art is characterized by the influence of popular mass culture in terms of theme and the techniques the artists employed. A famous example is Warhol's repetition, in garish colors, of the silk-screened image of Marilyn Monroe, or his detailed paintings of Campbell's soup cans. The Pop art movement has been seen alternately as a rejection of, or an expansion of, the modes of abstract expressionism, which remained a prevalent style of New York artists in the 1970s. At once academic (in that it is often difficult to decipher techniques) and designed by way of its subject matter to appeal to a wide audience, Pop art asserted, in much the same way the abstract expressionism did, a faith in the idea of artistic possibility. In some ways, it was characterized by anti-aestheticism, or by the rejection of the notion of controlling artistic principles. Ashbery's poem exhibits similar tendencies, exploring both the shortcomings and the possibilities of art.

Compare & Contrast

- **1520s:** In 1524, Italian explorer Giovanni da Verrazzano (c. 1485-c. 1528) explores the Atlantic coastline of North America. His journey takes him to New York Harbor (where the Verrazzano-Narrows Bridge is, having been named for the explorer) and north to Maine. Inhabitants of the largely uncultivated area are Native Americans.

1970s: New York City is a cultural center that promotes the arts in a variety of forms, including theater, painting, photography, literature, and music. At this time, punk rock is emerging as a new and rebellious form of artistic expression. Zoo York, graffiti art in the subway tunnel underneath New York City's Central Park Zoo, is also developing. New York City is Ashbery's adopted hometown, and his descriptions of life in the city play an important part in "Self-Portrait in a Convex Mirror."

Today: New York City remains an international cultural and artistic capital. The city hosts the "People's Poetry Gathering" in which New

Yorkers are encouraged to offer individual lines that form a larger poem. Following the September 11, 2001, terrorist attacks, this effort at communal poetry was employed to create a traveling exhibition featuring poems of 110 lines each, one line for each story of the World Trade Center towers destroyed in the attacks.

- **1520s:** Mannerism, as an artistic movement, is in its early phases. Parmigianino's works, including *Self-Portrait in a Convex Mirror* (1524) and *Madonna with the Long Neck* (1534-1540), along with the works of artists such as Rosso Fiorentino, including his *Descent from the Cross* (1521), exemplify this style. Mannerism is characterized by distortions in perspective, exaggerated physical features, disturbing compositions, and often unusual color choices. Given this definition, Ashbery's "Self-Portrait in a Convex Mirror" could be considered a Mannerist poem.

1970s: Conceptual art is becoming popular, and it is concerned primarily with the idea, or concept expressed, rather than with conventional modes of style or notions of aesthetics. Ashbery's "Self-Portrait in a Convex Mirror" could also be considered in this light, as it explores the ability of art to represent truth; it is, in many ways, *about* art itself.

Today: Notions about what constitutes art in the twenty-first century continue to shift. Nevertheless conceptual art remains fashionable: in 2005 Simon Starling exhibits his *Shedboatshed* a wooden shed that was turned into a boat, sailed down the Rhine River, and turned back into a shed.

- **1520s:** English-language poetry at this time is dictated by the conventions of the pastoral and lyric forms. Pastoral poetry exalts an idealized, simple world of shepherds and shepherdesses, and it expresses the joys of country life and laments romantic troubles. Lyric poetry of this period features the praising of love and nature, or often of God and spirituality. These types of poems are characterized by structured forms and rhyme schemes.

1970s: Poetry is influenced by artistic movements such as Surrealism, a cultural movement typically associated with the visual arts but also related to philosophy and literature. Surrealist works incorporate elements of surprise and of unexpected juxtapositions. Ashbery is writing at a time when many poets, Surrealists and otherwise, seek to resist traditional poetic movements and forms, and "Self-Portrait in a Convex Mirror" is an example of a work that is unique in its form and structure.

Today: Though modern poetry still shows resistance to form and convention, there has also been a revival of poetry crafted with attention to meter, formal rhyme schemes, and traditional structures, an a movement described as New Formalism. Critics sometimes describe it as a "closed" form that opposes or threatens the open, free verse poetry popular in many critical and academic circles.

Italian High Renaissance Art

The subject of Ashbery's poem is the painting by Parmigianino, *Self-Portrait in a Convex Mirror*. The painting was completed in 1524, during the end of the High Renaissance period (a short period of about twenty-five years, beginning at the end of the fifteenth century, and continuing through the beginning of the sixteenth century) of art in Italy and the beginning of the Mannerist period. During the High Renaissance, the highest achievements in painting were characterized by spatial harmony, exquisite arrangements of subjects, and proportions that were naturalistic and graceful. Examples of this period include such famous works as Leonardo da Vinci's (1452-1519) *Last Supper* (completed in 1498), Michelangelo's (1475-1564) *David* (completed in 1504), and Raphael's (1483-1520) *Transfiguration of Christ* (completed in 1520). At the time, however, a new movement, that which became known as Mannerism, was becoming prominent. In Mannerist works, artists such as Parmigianino, Benvenuto Cellini (1500-1571), and Georgio Vasari (1511-1574) distort perspective and depict figures with extremely exaggerated or unnatural features. Political and religious factors are cited as contributors to these dramatic shifts in the visual arts. Florence, the center of artistic creation in the region at the time, lost its political independence in 1512 and was now under the rule of the Medici family. Conditions of the population became miserable, and the city resented its loss of freedom. Concurrently, the Roman Catholic Church began to lose followers to Protestantism. When a member of the powerful Medici family became pope in 1523, political unrest and religious conflict fused. Armies that were supposedly loyal to the Roman Emperor Charles V but were actually not under control at all attacked Rome, under the auspices of addressing the pope's political maneuverings and manipulations. The distortions of Mannerism, then, are said to reflect the social, political, and religious chaos of the time. The disturbing effects of Mannerism stand in sharp contrast to the ordered, graceful, and beautiful imagery of the recent High Renaissance.

"Self-Portrait in a Convex Mirror" is perhaps Ashbery's most studied poem; many critics certainly refer to it as his most accessible. Reviewers often comment that the language in it is more straightforward than in his other poems, and that the subject of the poem remains consistent throughout. In 1979, poet, literary critic, and art historian David Shapiro explains in *John Ashbery: An Introduction to the Poetry*: "From the beginning of the poem to the end the poet reenacts both a meditation upon the painting ... and a meditation on the unfolding of his own vital poem." "Self-Portrait in a Convex Mirror" is often described as unique in its ability to verbally convey the visceral, visual impact of the painting, rather than simply describing the physical details of the image, or discussing the manner by which it was created.

In a *Journal of Modern Literature* essay published in 1976, shortly after the publication of Ashbery's poem, Fred Moramarco comments that Ashbery is able "to explore the verbal implications of painterly space, to capture the verbal nuances of Parmigianino's fixed and distorted image. The poem virtually resonates or extends the painting's meaning. It transforms visual impact to verbal precision." Moramarco goes on to explore the way Ashbery attempts to "record verbally the emotional truth contained in Parmigianino's painting." Later critics have reassessed the poem's achievements in this area. Travis Looper, in a 1992 essay in *Papers on Language and Literature* suggests that Ashbery's poem is a study of the failure of language, of the inability of verbal expression to accurately capture meaning. Looper asserts that Ashbery is aware "even as he writes the words of the poem, that the signs are themselves paltry substitutes of the object-realities he would describe." Nevertheless, Looper goes on, the poet continues to use words as signifiers even though he is aware of their inadequacy, otherwise Ashbery would be "undermining the poem even as he writes it. Rather, in human fashion, he persists in that which is ultimately hopeless."

Other critics agree that the poem is *about* representation. Richard Stamelman, in his 1984 essay for *New Literary History*, maintains that Ashbery emphasizes the differences between Parmigianino's act of self-portrayal and the way Ashbery represents himself in the poem. Commenting that Ashbery approaches art from a postmodern standpoint, Stamelman identifies Ashbery's position as one in which "painting and poetry can represent nothing other than their own difficult, often thwarted efforts at representation." A more positive description of Ashbery's views on the possibilities and limitations of artistic representation is offered by David Herd in his 2000 book, *John Ashbery and American Poetry*. Herd observes that in "Self-Portrait in a Convex Mirror," "Ashbery's poetic, like Emerson's 'American Scholar,' but unlike Parmigianino's painting, leads the reader beyond the confines and conventions of artistic practice and into an encounter with their own experience."

What Do I Read Next?

- "Song of Myself," by Walt Whitman, is available in *Leaves of Grass: The Original 1855 Edition* (reprinted 2007). Like Ashbery,American poet Walt Whitman was known for his unconventional poetic structures, his cataloging of human experiences, an often rambling style, and his explorations of the soul and the relationship between the body and the soul.

- "The Over-Soul" (1841), by Ralph Waldo Emerson, is available in *Emerson's Essays* (1981). The prominent scholar and critic Harold

Bloom has observed that Ashbery's poetry is highly influenced by the philosophy of American Transcendentalism, which is explored and explained in Emerson's essay.

- *A Worldly Country: New Poems* (2007), by John Ashbery, features Ashbery'smost recent poetic compositions. The poems are playful in tone but cover serious themes such as old age and death.

- *Parmigianino* (2006), by David Ekserdjian, contains previously unpublished drawings by Parmigianino as well as a new painting. Ekserdjian analyzes the significance of Parmigianino's works, and he also discusses the painter's artistic development while praising his artistic achievements.

- *Tales of E. T. A. Hoffmann* (1972) is a collection of short stories by E. T. A. Hoffmann. Ashbery makes reference in "Self-Portrait in a Convex Mirror" to the short-story characters created by the science fiction/fantasy writer Hoffmann (1776-1822).

Sources

Ashbery, John, "Self-Portrait in a Convex Mirror," in *Selected Poems*, Penguin, 1986, pp. 188-204.

Ashbery, John, and Mark Ford, *John Ashbery in Conversation with Mark Ford*, Between the Lines, 2003.

Emerson, Ralph Waldo, "The Over-Soul," in *Emerson's Essays*, Harper Perennial, 1981, pp. 188-211

Hartt, Frederick, "Part Four: The Renaissance," in *Art: A History of Painting, Sculpture, Architecture*, Vol. 2, 3rd edition, Prentice-Hall, 1989, pp. 627-44.

Herd, David, "John Ashbery in Conversation: The Communicative Value of *Self-Portrait in a Convex Mirror*," in *John Ashbery and American Poetry*, Manchester University Press, 2000, pp. 144-78.

Kalstone, David, "*Self-Portrait in a Convex Mirror*," in *Bloom's Modern Critical Views: John Ashbery*, edited by Harold Bloom, Chelsea House Publishers, 1985, pp. 91-114.

Leckie, Ross, "Art, Mimesis, and John Ashbery's 'Self-Portrait in a Convex Mirror'," in *Essays in Literature*, Vol. XIX, No. 1, Spring 1992, pp. 114-31.

Looper, Travis, "Ashbery's 'Self-Portrait,'" in *Papers on Language and Literature*, Vol. 28, No. 4, Fall 1992, pp. 451-56.

Moramarco, Fred, "John Ashbery and Frank O'Hara: The Painterly Poets," in *Journal of Modern Literature*, Vol. 5, No. 3, September 1976, pp. 436-62.

Plato, *Meno*, translated by. R. W. Sharples, Aris & Phillips, 1986.

Shapiro, David, "Prolegomenon: The Mirror Staged" in *John Ashbery: An Introduction to the Poetry*, Columbia University Press, 1979, pp. 177-78.

Stamelman, Richard, "Critical Reflections: Poetry and Art Criticism in Ashbery's 'Self-Portrait in a Convex Mirror,'" in *New Literary History*, Vol. 15, No. 3, Spring 1984, pp. 607-30.

Further Reading

Bloom, Harold, ed., *Modern Critical Views: John Ashbery*, Chelsea House Publishers, 1985.

> Bloom's collection of essays explores Ashbery's poetic aims, as well as his thematic, stylistic, and structural approaches to poetry.

Criswell, David, *The Rise and Fall of the Holy Roman Empire: From Charlemagne to Napolean*, PublishAmerica, 2005.

> This book details the power struggles between emperors and popes throughout the duration of the Holy Roman Empire, providing both a church history as well as a secular history of the time period. This study provides the historical context for understanding the political climate in Italy during the 1500s. The politics of this time greatly impacted the endeavors of artists, such as Parmigianino, whose work inspired Ashbery's poem.

Franklin, David, *The Art of Parmigianino*, Yale University Press, 2004.

> Franklin discusses Parmigianino's inspirations as well as his artistic struggles, and explores the artist's

desire to convey, through his art, complex ideas. The book additionally contains numerous photographs of the artist's works.

Friedlaender, W., *Mannerism and Anti-Mannerism in Italian Painting*, Columbia University Press, 1990.

Friedlaender, one of the world's most prominent art historians, details the elements of the Mannerist movement, discussing it as a reaction against High Renaissance ideals. Friedlaender additionally studies the artistic reaction against Mannerism, that is, the Anti-Mannerist movement.

Heffernan, James A. W., *The Poetics of Ekphrasis: From Homer to Ashbery*, University of Chicago Press, 2004.

Heffernan studies ekphrasis (the practice of describing works of visual art) as a struggle between two modes of representation and discusses Ashbery's work within this larger framework.

Kraut, Richard, ed., *The Cambridge Companion to Plato*, Cambridge University Press, 1992.

This collection of essays examines Plato's views on such subjects as knowledge, reality, and poetry, and places Plato's writings within the context of the intellectual and social background of his time.

CPSIA information can be obtained
at www.ICGtesting.com
Printed in the USA
BVOW08s1913140917
494782BV00009B/233/P